CW01306264

APY
cure

2

RUNNING THERAPY

The New DEPRESSION cure:

Fight Depression Naturally, Regain Your Life and Live a Happier Healthier Life

(Natural Cures Book 1)

Theophile Gray

Copyright 2015 Theophile Gray - All rights reserved
This document is geared towards providing exact and reliable information in regards to the topic and issue covered. The publication is sold with the idea that the publisher is not required to render accounting, officially permitted, or otherwise, qualified services. If advice is necessary, legal or professional, a practiced individual in the profession should be ordered.

From a Declaration of Principles which was accepted and approved equally by a Committee of the American Bar Association and a Committee of Publishers and Associations.

In no way is it legal to reproduce, duplicate, or transmit any part of this document in either electronic means or in printed format. Recording of this publication is strictly prohibited and any storage of this document is not allowed unless with written permission from the publisher. All rights reserved.

The information provided herein is stated to be truthful and consistent, in that any liability, in terms of inattention or otherwise, by any usage or abuse of any policies, processes, or directions contained within is the solitary and utter responsibility of the recipient reader. Under no circumstances will any legal responsibility or blame be held against the publisher for any reparation, damages, or monetary loss due to the information herein, either directly or indirectly.

The information herein is offered for informational purposes solely, and is universal as so. The presentation of the information is without contract or any type of guarantee assurance.

The trademarks that are used are without any consent, and the publication of the trademark is without permission or backing by the trademark owner. All trademarks and brands within this book are for clarifying purposes only and are the owned by the owners themselves, not affiliated with this document.

Table of contents

1. Introduction   6

2. What is Depression?   8

3. Causes of depression and how to handle it   14

4. Running therapy for depression   22

5. The benefits of running therapy   28

6. Combine running therapy with regular therapy   33

7. Twenty steps to combat depression   37

8. Frequently asked questions   44

1. Introduction

"When you laugh the world laughs with you and when you cry you cry alone."

Depression is a condition which has long been misunderstood and been made light of. While there is a greater understanding of depression now there are still many misgivings about this particular health issue. One of the main differences that mental health issues have in comparison to other ailments is that on the surface the person may look healthy and normal. However, once you scratch the surface a very different picture will emerge and the person with depression may need urgent attention and care.

This e-book aims to provide the reader a concise background on depression and how it can be managed. This e-book also discusses how running therapy helps people recover from depression whether used on its own or with other more standard and mainstream treatments (medicines and therapies). Furthermore, this e-book also looks into other non-medicinal alternatives that can help us ease out of depression.

Chapter 2 looks at how depression is defined, what its main symptoms are and what are the main types of depression that can be diagnosed. Chapter 3 then follows on and looks at some of the reasons depression may appear in some people's lives and how family and friends can help them cope with it. These two chapters are sources of basic information about depression.

Chapters 4 and 5 look at running therapy and how it has a positive influence on people with depression. These chapters look at what running therapy is, how it affects our body and mind and in what ways it is beneficial for people who suffer depression.

Chapter 6 discusses how running therapy even combined with other more mainstream forms of treatment for depression can help people.

Chapter 7 looks at twenty other things that can help weaken depression in people with out the taking of heavy medication.

2. What is Depression?

"Courage doesn't always roar. Sometimes courage is the quiet voice at the end of the day saying 'I will try again tomorrow.' "(Mary Anne Radmacher, American author and artist)

This chapter introduces us to what depression is, how we can detect it through its many varied symptoms and also discusses the different types of depression.

Defining depression

Depression is more than just getting the blues, feeling down in the dumps, being anti social, feeling as if there is a grey cloud over your head or a burden on your shoulders that you just can't bear. It's more than just something in your head as people are prone to tell you.. Depression is a real medical condition that needs to be treated with as much care as any other medical problem. Depression is known to be caused by a complex change in the brain chemistry.

Currently, one in five women and one in twelve men around the world suffer from depression at some point in their lives. Depression can strike you down at any particular point in your life; it does not discriminate in terms of age, class, career and ethnic background. Depression will affect every aspect of life whether it is your family life, friendships, marriage, career, finances, or social life. Furthermore, if you have had a bout of depression once its very possible that it can re-occur. The impact of depression can be particularly devastating if paired with other medical problems such as diabetes, stroke, a heart condition and cancer.

While a large number of people who suffer from depression, do so silently as their problem has not been diagnosed, evidence shows that once the problem is detected it can be dealt with quickly and successfully. Depression can be dealt with great speed particularly if it is detected in its initial stages.

Symptoms of depression

Sometimes it is difficult to pinpoint depression in a person because they have a range of symptoms that are physical, behavioral, thoughts and feelings related. However if you feel you have some of the symptoms listed below it is best to go to a healthcare professional and discuss them.

- **Physical symptoms:** Feeling tired or sapped of energy; having aches and pains around the body, have a change in appetite (eat too little or too much), sleep patterns may change (may sleep too little or too much) and you may have sexual problems.

- **Behavioral symptoms:** Becoming socially withdrawn, taking sick leave off work, avoiding friends and acquaintances, drinking or taking drugs or attempting to harm yourself.

- **Thought related symptoms:** Being mentally clouded, unable to concentrate, unable to make decisions, unable to remember or understand things going on.

- **Feelings related symptoms:** You may also be feeling sad, guilty, hopeless and angry.

Types of depression

There are several different types of depression that can be diagnosed, some of them are mild and others are more severe. The word depression is actually just an umbrella term for a number of different forms, from major depression to atypical depression to dysthymia.

1. **Major depression:** In fact, about 7 percent of the U.S. adult population has this debilitating mental health condition at any given time, according to the National Institute of Mental Health (NIMH). If you're experiencing major depression, you may feel and see symptoms of extreme sadness, hopelessness, lack of energy, irritability, trouble concentrating, changes in sleep or eating habits, feelings of guilt, physical pain, and thoughts of death or suicide — and for an official diagnosis, your symptoms must last for more than two weeks. In some instances, a person might only experience one episode of major depression, but the condition tends to recur throughout a person's life.

2. **Dysthymia:** This is one of the more widespread form of depressions and a relatively mild one. This depression causes a low mood over a long period of time sometimes months or years. People can go about doing what they normally do, fulfilling their day to day work but at a sub-optimal level. They may feel sad, have trouble concentrating, suffer from fatigue, or have changes in their eating and sleep habits. People with

dysthymia may also be at risk for episodes of major depression. This depression can be treated through therapy rather than medication; however, some evidence shows that a combination of therapy and medicine may work best.

3. **Persistent Depressive Disorder:** A depression that lasts over 2 years, involving symptoms that come and go in severity. The key is that the symptoms must be present at least two years

4. **Post-partum Depression:** More than four fifths (85 %) of new mothers feel sad after their baby is born. However, only one in six women have depression that is serious enough to be diagnosed; sadly, the rest of the new mothers suffer silently. This form of depression is characterized by sadness, fatigue, loneliness, hopelessness, suicidal thoughts, fears of hurting the baby, and general disconnect from the child. It can occur anywhere from weeks to months after childbirth. It needs quick diagnosis and medical care through a combination of talking therapy and drug therapy.

5. **Seasonal Affective Disorder (SAD):** Many people find themselves suffering from winter blues and seem to think its the norm rather than going to the doctor and getting diagnosed with SAD. SAD is characterized by anxiety, irritability, fatigue and weight gain. This type of depression typically occurs in winter due to less natural sunlight. Symptoms are usually mild, though they can be severe at times. This depression starts in early winter and gets better in the spring, and it can be treated with artificial light treatment. Artificial light which can be placed on your work desk or at home to help you get the light you need.

6. **Atypical depression:** Unlike major depression, a common sign of atypical depression is a sense of heaviness in the arms and legs. However, a study published in the Archives of General Psychiatry found that over-sleeping and over-eating are the two most important symptoms for diagnosing atypical depression. People with the condition may also gain weight, be irritable, and have relationship problems.

7. **Psychotic Depression:** This type of depression is characterized by delusions, false sights or sounds, known as hallucinations that don't typically get associated with depression. According to the National Alliance on Mental Illness, about one in five people with depression have episodes so severe that they see or hear things that are not there. Treatment may require a combination of antidepressant and anti-psychotic medications.

8. **Bipolar Disorder:** If you suffer from periods of extreme lows followed by periods of extreme highs, you could be suffering from a bipolar disorder. Symptoms of mania include high energy, excitement, racing thoughts, and poor judgment. Bipolar disorder has four basic subtypes: bipolar I (characterized by at least one manic episode); bipolar II (characterized by hypomanic episodes milder — along with depression); cyclothymic disorder and other specified bipolar and related disorder. People with bipolar disorder are typically treated with drugs called mood stabilizers.

9. **Premenstrual Dysphoric Disorder:** Premenstrual dysphoric disorder (PMDD) is a type of depression that affects women

during the second half of their menstrual cycles. Symptoms include depression, anxiety, and mood swings. Unlike premenstrual syndrome (PMS), which affects up to nine in ten (85%) of women and has milder symptoms, PMDD affects about 5% of women and is much more severe. Treatment may include a combination of depression drugs as well as talk and nutrition therapies.

3. Causes of depression and how to handle it

"It does not matter how slowly you go so long as you do not stop."
(Confucius, Chinese philosopher)

This chapter will look at the numerous reasons that may trigger depression or make it significantly worse. This chapter will also look at some important ways of looking after someone who has depression.

What causes depression?

Depression is caused by a number of complex chemical processes but can be triggered by a number of reasons. We are going to look at some of the many reasons which can act as a trigger to depression or make existing depression worse.

Abuse: Past physical, sexual, or emotional abuse can **cause depression** later in life. This is particularly so if the abuse has been carried out during your childhood - depression, anxiety and guilt can be a life-long battle.

Conflict: Depression in someone who has the vulnerability to develop depression may result from personal conflicts or disputes with family or friends. Children who have been brought up in a conflict-ridden house may develop depression. Someone who is going through marital difficulty or is in the process of divorce is more prone to depression. Someone who is unhappy at work or doesn't get along with his or her boss may suffer from depression.

Death or a loss: Sadness or grief from the death or loss of a loved one, though natural, may increase the risk of depression. For most people this can be treated through time passing and talking therapy.

Gender: Women get depressed more often than men. Perhaps men are less likely to talk about their feelings and more likely to deal with them by drinking heavily or becoming aggressive. Women are more likely to have the double stress of having to work and look after children.

Genes: A family history of depression may increase the risk. It's thought that depression is a complex trait that may be inherited across generations, although the genetics of psychiatric disorders are not as simple or straightforward as other *purely* genetic diseases.

Important events in life: Major events in life that may actually be good events such as starting a new job, graduating, or getting married can lead to depression. So can moving, losing a job or income, getting divorced, or retiring.

Medications: Some drugs, such as Accutane (used to treat acne), the antiviral drug interferon-alpha, and corticosteroids, can increase your risk of depression.

Personal problems: Problems such as social isolation due to other mental illnesses or being cast out of a family or social group, losing a job or facing financial problem can lead to depression. Research shows that the wider a person's social network the less likely the chance of his or her suffering from depression.

Serious illnesses: Sometimes depression co-exists with a major illness or is a reaction to the illness. It could be diabetes, a heart condition, stroke, or cancer and as a result of those a person may sink into depression. This is a very serious matter as that person may not be able to take care of himself physically and mentally when they really need to. This is when the depression sufferer may need the most help to get himself out of two different but serious health problems.

Substance abuse: Nearly 30% of people with substance abuse problems also have major or clinical depression.

How a family will cope with depression

Depression is a medical condition that will affect every aspect of the sufferer's life. While their family members and friends won't necessarily feel as bad as them they will still be very much affected by this problem. This part of the chapter will look at what family and friends can do to help a depression sufferer and carry on with their own lives.

Stand in the other person's shoes

One of the first things to do when dealing with a family member or friend who has depression is to try and see things from their point of view. Try and understand that it is hard for people with depression to function normally. Depression can affect every aspect of the sufferer's life - ability to work, ability to run a house, look after themselves and their families. They often exercise, socializing with friends, eating and sleeping properly or even looking after their personal hygiene.

It's important to understand that people with depression often feel overwhelmed by the sheer number of things they are feeling. They may be feeling, sadness, grief, guilt and may have a very low self-esteem. Most importantly they probably feel guilt at the difficulty their family and friends have to face because of them.

Stand in your own shoes

While it is very important to look after a depressed family member or friend and understand their point of view, it is also very important to look at yourselves and see how you feel about the situation. You may be feeling a range of emotions when dealing with this problem with a family member or friend; the most common are listed below:

- **Anger:** You may feel anger at them, particularly so, if you feel they are being lazy, or weak or are not fighting hard enough to get out of depression. You may feel that you are burdened down with everything and have to pitch in on behalf of your family member or friends. The important thing is to be patient and not show your anger to that person.

- **Depression:** Watching a family member or a close friend go through and trying to help them may eventually lead you into depression. But this should be a big no no. You are there to help them and not to sink into depression yourself.

- **Embarrassment:** You may also find yourself feeling embarrassed at your family member or friend. You may think that they are being weak, lazy or just plain whinny. But that is not the case, once again, you need patience, fortitude and most importantly you need to show the depression sufferer that you are with them for the long-haul.

- **Frustration:** You may feel frustration because you might not know what the person with depression is feeling. You may not understand why that person is not pulling their weight at work or helping you at home. You may seem them managing better at work and then letting completely go of themselves at work.

- **Guilt:** There can be an over-riding sense of guilt amongst family members and friends because they feel they haven't done enough for the person who is going through depression. But the only way to help the person in depression is to overcome guilt and get on with things.

- **Impatience:** You want your family member or friend to get better or start leading a normal life. You so badly want your life back and their life to be back to normal that your impatience is hardly masked. The important thing to do here is to show patience because it may take some time for the person to get out of their depression.

- **Sadness:** Friends and family member watching someone they know or love go through depression often find it a painful and sad affair. They may find it sad because they know their loved one is struggling and suffering. They may also find it painful because they think of the life that their loved one is missing out on.

How to provide the right kind of support

There are many things that can be done to help a loved one or a friend going through depression. The most important thing is to let them know that you are there and will give support. But its also necessary to learn more about depression, show patience and help them out where you can. However, its also important to understand that you cannot help them out on your own and will need to realize your own limitation. Most importantly, you cannot interrupt your own life and need to carry on with things that are important to you.

- **We stand together approach:** It is important to let the depression sufferer know that he/she doesn't stand alone. Its important for them to know that despite the pain and misery they feel there are people around them who will help and stand by in any other way they can. This help may be in the shape of proving them company, giving them moral support, financial support or perhaps attending their therapy talks or support groups with them.

- **Educate yourself:** If you want to help someone with depression then it would be a good idea to arm yourself with knowledge about the condition. If you are knowledgeable about depression then you will be able to avoid missteps and misunderstandings and will be able to help your friend or loved one more.

- **Be patient:** Patience is a virtue and particularly so when you want to help someone who is suffering from depression. By showing patience towards someone who has depression you are signaling to them that you are in for the long run, that you will stand by them no matter what. Patience in a sense is able to give hope. Hope is a very powerful tool when someone is suffering from depression.

- **Be a listener:** When someone close to you is in depression try and curb the need to give advice. You may mean it in a well-meaning way but it may not go down well. Even if you think the advice is harmless and beneficial. It is far more important to give the sufferer you company and listen carefully to what they have say.

- **Carry on with your life:** While you may be affected by the depression of a family member or friend and are giving them the required support it is important to remember what is important in your life. You life has to go on, routine matters need to be taken care of and you still have to enjoy the things you always did i.e. hobbies, socializing, work, looking after your family. You may feel guilty for getting on with your life but that is perhaps the best way of being able to help the depression sufferers.

- **Treat yourself well:** While it is important to look after someone with depression it is also important that you get enough rest and treat yourself well. Its important that you get out with your friends, get regular exercise, treat yourself to a spa, or go to a movie. If you don't look after yourself how will you be able to look after others?

- **Understand your limitations:** You need to understand clearly to what extent you can help your loved one or friend suffering from depression. If you can visit once every other day then do that effectively, if you can only go with him/her to therapy session then do that wholeheartedly. If you can take him/her out on the weekends that is fine as well. Don't feel guilty for what you can't do, do what you can wholeheartedly.

- **Plan out positive things:** It is important, to stand together and plan good and positive things. Going out for walks, planning dinners, seeing a movie, or going on short breaks together. All these positive things will help the depression sufferer.

4. Running therapy for depression

"It always seems impossible until it's done." (Nelson Mandela, South African anti-apartheid leader)

This chapter looks at what, if any, evidence is present on the beneficial effect running therapy has on depression sufferers. We have long been hearing about the beneficial effects of exercise for people suffering from anxiety and depression. We will now take a look at what running therapy can do for people who are suffering from depression (mild to severe depression).

What is running therapy?

'Running therapy' may sound very sophisticated but the idea is simple enough - you put on a pair of shorts and an old t-shirt, you lace up your running shoes, step outside and start running. Begin easy and gradually build up your running routine. For example, the first few days run ten minutes in total with a small breaks in between; run for five minutes then rest for two minutes and then run for five minutes. Remember to keep a water bottle with you and stay hydrated. Gradually start running for fifteen minutes, then twenty minutes, then half an hour and more if possible and remember to take a break and hydrate yourself where necessary.

Release those endorphins

When you exercise (in this case when you run), your body releases chemicals called endorphins. These endorphins interact with the receptors in your brain that reduce pain and act as sedatives. Endorphins are manufactured in your brain, spinal cord, and many other parts of your body and are released in response to neurotransmitters. The neuron receptors endorphins bind to are the same ones that bind some pain medicines. Endorphins trigger a positive feeling in the body. For example, the feeling that follows a run or workout is often described as "euphoric." That feeling, known as a "runner's high," can be accompanied by a positive and healthy outlook on life.

Prevention of neuron loss

Another possibility is the effect of exercise-triggered growth factors, such as brain-derived neurotrophic factor, which are associated with the growth of new neurons – a key point, since depression is thought to be associated with neuron loss in certain brain areas. There is a large quantity of anecdotal evidence that suggests that exercise generally and running in particular is able to help people who have mild to moderate depression get out of depression and then continue to stay healthy.

What does research say

This sub-section will now attempt to cover some of the recent key research that looks at the effect of running therapy on people with depression. All of the research studies except one have been carried out on men and women who have depression. The last study mentioned in this sub-section has been carried out on mice who show symptoms of depression but strengthens the hypothesis of all the other studies cited. The main hypothesis here is that running therapy has a positive effect on people suffering with light or moderate levels of depression.

Archives of Internal Medicine (1999), published a study which divided 156 men and women with depression into three groups. The first group took part in an aerobic exercise program, the second group took the Zoloft, and the third group took part in the exercise program and too Zoloft. At the 16-week mark, depression had eased in all three groups. About 60%–70% of the people in all groups no longer had major depression. In fact, group scores on in terms of depression ratings were essentially the same. This suggests that people who need or wish to avoid drugs, exercise might be an acceptable substitutes. However, the swiftest response occurred in the group taking antidepressants, and that it can be difficult to stay motivated to exercise when you're depressed.

A follow-up to that study found that the exercise effects lasted longer than those of antidepressants. Researchers checked in with 133 of the original patients six months after the first study ended. People who exercised regularly after completing the study, regardless of which treatment they were on originally, were less likely to relapse into depression.

A similar study in 2004 compared running and psychotherapy. For 10 weeks, participants were randomly assigned to run for 20 minutes three times a week, attend one 60-minute therapy session every week or do both. All three groups displayed a significant reduction in depression, with no meaningful differences between them, and positive benefits were still present at a four-month follow-up.

Dr. Andrea Dunn conducted a study at the Cooper Research Institute in Dallas, Texas (2005) found that patients who did an equivalent of 35 minutes walking, six days per week, experienced a significant reduction (47%) in their depression. This study, shows that three hours of exercise a week reduces the symptoms of mild to moderate depression as effectively as antidepressants.

Dr. Guy Faulkner, head of the exercise psychology group (University of Toronto) and founding editor of the journal Mental Health and Physical Activity, agrees with the above and points to studies in which even mild walking helps alleviate depression. Whatever different mechanisms are at work during exercise, the precise combination that makes any given patient feel better is likely to be "highly individual-specific," he says.

A Swedish study offers yet another fascinating insight into the way running and exercise helps us out of depression. Researchers induced depression-like behavior in mice by inducing stress in them through exposing them to loud noises and flashing lights for five weeks. The stress caused increased production of kynurenine (a molecule) in the liver, which travels through the bloodstream to the brain. Kynurenine is associated with brain inflammation and neuron death. Patients with a variety of mental illnesses tend to have elevated levels of kynurenine.

But when the same experiments were repeated with mice that were physically fit, less kynurenine entered the brain. Exercise causes muscles to produce a protein called PGC-1alpha1, which produces an enzyme transforming kynurenine into kynurenic acid. Kynurenic acid can't cross the blood-brain barrier, so it's unable to create trouble in the brain. As a result, the fit mice were less likely to develop depression despite exposure to the lights and noises. While there are huge differences between men and mice this study further strengthens the hypothesis that exercise is beneficial for people with depression regardless of what kind of treatment they receive.

Conclusion

According to the studies mentioned in the chapter above:
- Running therapy works as well as medicine for some people to reduce symptoms of depression;
- The effects of running therapy in terms of keeping depression at bay can be long lasting.
- Running therapy can be most effective in combating depression amongst people who have light to moderate levels of depression.
- However, although exercise has a positive effect for most people, some studies show that for some, exercise may not

have a positive effect on depression may or may not make a strong impact on long-term mental health - this is particularly for people with severe depression.

5. The benefits of running therapy

"I am a slow walker, but I never walk back."

This chapter discusses the benefits of running therapy for those who have been through or are going through depression. Running therapy here merely means putting on a pair of good running shoes, changing into an old t-shirt and shorts and hitting the pavement. As we will see below that there are numerous physical, mental and emotional benefits of adopting the running therapy where you suffer from depression or don't.

No medication reliance

The main benefit of engaging with running therapy to counteract depression is that there are no side effects similar to those with taking medication (anti-depressants). One of the problems with treating depression is that the person suffering from it can often be over drugged. Running is exercise out in the fresh air, it gets you some much needed physical exercise, which releases endorphins which makes the mind feel happy, positive and more able to take what is around them.

Cost effective treatment

Running proves to be a cost effective form of treatment for depression. When we think of depression or any other mental health issue, we think of lots of trips to the psychologist or psychiatrist and a long list of pills to take. All of this points towards lots of money being spent on treatment which sometimes continue for years. Running therapy is the complete opposite with the running being free and done in a pair of old shorts and a t-shirt - the most expensive item being a pair of decent running shoes!

Running with a friend

While lots of people carry out their running therapy in solitude and enjoy the silence, being on their own and the peace and quiet it brings; running can also be done with a friend. Running for those in depression can be a good way to get out and socialise, either you run with a friend or a family member or join a local group once or twice a month to run together. Running together can also ensure friendship or comradeships developing over time. This is an important factor for someone who is in depression as it allows them to socialise and meet people.

Being out in the open

Running also ensures that you start to connect with nature and that you are no longer spending days cooped up in the house and being miserable. Movement outside helps bring further movement, once you are out and about running you may actually for a time being be able to control or halt your negative thoughts and just concentrate on putting one foot before the other. Without a phone, pager or laptop you may just be able to disconnect yourself from the world for a little while.

Soaking vitamin D

Running out in the open ensure that you get some vitamin D which is a much needed antidote for depression. Better than pill popping vitamin D and multi-vitamins, soaking natural sunlight does wonders for the body, mind and soul. Generally being out and about in day light is good for people particularly those who are going through depression.

Therapy for life

Running therapy can be considered a form of self-therapy for life. Its a form of therapy that you are able to regulate and decide how much, how little, when and where you need this therapy. Running can help you empty your mind, sort out your thoughts, tackle your problems head on and see everything in perspective. There is no cost for this therapy, no negative side effects, no one hour clock running for the therapy session. In other words there are no limitations to this form of therapy.

Running strengthens the brain

It prevents stress by beating it to pulp and it reduces muscle tension which reduces anxiety as it interrupts the mental feedback loop of anxiety within the brain. Running slows cognitive decline and strengthens your capacity for and rate of learning. It balances and regulates neurotransmitters in the brain to promote focus, make the brain alert and improving self-esteem.

A form of meditation

Running can be considered a form of meditation - primarily for the positive effect it has on your mind. It is an act of putting one foot in front of the other again and again and again. This continuous act, the certainty of doing this countless times helps us to focus. Numerous accounts of runners in general and people with depression who run allows us to understand that the act of running helps them empty their mind. It allows them to focus on one thing alone (the act of running) and leave everything else behind.

Sense of achievement

Often people coping with depression suffer from a low self-esteem. Through running, gradually building up their stamina, running longer, running faster, being able to participate in and complete races, people with depression experience a sense of joy, pride and achievement. Being able to run also acts as a metaphor for being able to get on with life and overcome depression.

Keep in check health problems

In addition to all the above benefits connected with running therapy two additional important ones are: keeping your weight in check and avoiding obesity; keeping a healthy heart with the exercise; and keeping your joints working. Often when you start suffering from depression a number of additional health problems crop up - obesity, cardiovascular problems and limbs hurting (particularly in the case of atypical depression)

6. Combine running therapy with regular therapy

"Courage is not having the strength to go on; it is going on when you don't have the strength." (Theodore Roosevelt, 26th President of the United States)

This chapter will discuss how running therapy combined with regular therapy can help someone with depression and fight depression more effectively. It will also discuss why regular therapy is needed in addition to running therapy.

Looking at different research that has been done across the world the last few decades, the positive effect of exercise on people with depression is quite encouraging. In groups where exercise has been given as a treatment with and without medication and/or talking therapy the patient has improved. However, healthcare professionals and therapists have been cautious in terms of prescribing running therapy as treatment for depression. Healthcare professionals and therapists still feel that medicines and talking therapies cannot be substituted by running therapies.

It has been mentioned a number of research studies that running therapy is beneficial in cases of light to moderate depression. Exercise in general and running in particular has been able to help people get out of depression combined with more mainstream treatments. Here is why we feel that mainstream (medication and talking therapy) depression treatment is important in combination with the running therapy.

Anti-depressant medication

When depression is at a high/severe level or if a person suffers from clinical depression and is unable to get out of bed or feel generally weighted down in their life, it is crucial to get medication to cope on a day to day basis. Medication often helps a person get out of their bed or arm chair at best and helps them stay alive at worse. Medication is at times the only resort when depression turns out severe. In order to run you need to be able to get out of bed and start walking around first. If you can't move or find yourself lying in bed most of the day what good would running be.

Talking therapy

Often when suffering from a moderate to severe level of depression, or order to reach a point where you can start thinking positively or evenly where you start looking after yourself, eating properly, sleeping properly and starting to consider exercise as a possibility, you need to change the way you think. In certain cases its only when you change the way you think you are able to get up and go for a run. However, you may find that once you start running that may also help change the way you think or perhaps bring in a positive change at a faster rate.

Intake of chemical required

At times, particularly where a person has clinical depression, there is a real need for an intake of certain chemicals which the body is not producing or is not producing enough of. Its the initially administering of these chemicals which allows a person to improve to a level where they can start taking initiatives on their own. The initiatives may be small like going for a walk or run, or considerably larger ones where you move out into your own place or getting a job.

A mixture of medicine and therapy

At times a cocktail of medication and talking therapies may be required to bring a person to a level where they are able to partake in simple things such as living on their own, taking up hobbies, reading books and starting to take part in the running therapy. For some people its a cocktail of treatments which need to be exercised before they are able to take part in normal physical and mental activities. So sometimes a lot of work needs to be done before a person can reach the stage where running therapy does them any good.

Overview: From this chapter we would like you to take the view that while running is generally beneficial for patients who have light to moderate depression, its mostly taken in addition with a one or two other forms of treatment. However, there has been anecdotal evidence where people have weaned themselves off from medication by following a running regime. However, first we need to conduct more research on exactly what kind of an effect and to what extent it can help depression

7. Twenty steps to combat depression

"Success is not final, failure is not fatal: It is the courage to continue that counts". (Winston Churchill, former Prime Minister of the United Kingdom)

This chapter introduces readers to twenty additional (non-pharmaceutical) steps which they can follow through in addition to the running therapy to combat depression. Most of these steps might seem obvious and very much part of your everyday lie but they will make a considerable difference to your depression.

1. **Recognize your need for help:** The first step toward combating depression is realizing that you have depression. It is important to recognize that it is not normal to feel low, unhappy or worthless for months at a time. Its also important to recognize that something can be done about these negative thoughts. Once you have acknowledged that you have depression, then you know that you need to tackle it. This first point is more geared towards men as they are more prone to keeping a stiff upper lip and not voicing their concerns.

2. **Don't keep it to yourself:** A problem shared is a problem halved - you have probably heard of this saying. If you've had some bad news, or a major upset, tell someone close to you - tell them how you feel. You may need to talk (and maybe cry)

about it more than once. This is part of the mind's natural way of healing. You need to know that its okay to share bad news and you will be no less strong for it - in fact you will be much more stronger and courageous for sharing.

3. **Seek professional help:** It may sound obvious but do seek professional help once you realize you have depression. The right type of therapist and therapy can do wonders for you. Its important to remember that there is no shame in seeking help and no weakness or flaw in you for going through depression. Luckily in this day and age we have a range of therapies that could help someone with depression.

4. **Do something:** If you feel you are in depression then you need to do something, anything. Get out of doors for some exercise, even if only for a walk. This will help you to keep physically fit, and will help you sleep. Even if you can't work, it's good to keep active. This could be housework, do-it-yourself (even as little as changing a light bulb), or any activity that is part of your normal routine. You could even re-visit your hobbies and start to get busy in that.

5. **Eat well:** You may feel like eating too little or eating too much but you need to make sure that you are eating just right. Try to eat regularly. Depression can make you lose weight and run short of vitamins that will only make you feel worse. Fresh fruit and vegetables are particularly helpful and lots of water. On the other hand depression can also make you indulge in comfort eating - eating the wrong types of food - too much fatty foods and carbohydrates.

6. **Avoid alcohol:** Try not to sort out your depression through drinking. Alcohol actually makes depression worse. While it may make you feel better for a short while, but it doesn't last. Drinking can stop you dealing with important problems and from getting the right help. It's also bad for your physical health and can lead to weight gain and a host of other problems.

7. **Keep away from drugs:** While some drugs can help you to relax, there is now evidence that regular use, particularly in teenagers and adults, can bring on depression. So if you already have depression then you may get yourself further into depression if you indulge in substance abuse.

8. **Use the healing power of sleep:** If you can't sleep, try not to worry about it. Settle down with some relaxing music or television while you're lying in bed. Your body will get a chance to rest and, with your mind occupied, you may feel less anxious and find it easier to get some sleep. However, don't overdo on sleep, some depression suffers find themselves sleeping half or more than half the day - that is a definite no no.

9. **Soak up some vitamin D:** One of the things that you can do to draw yourself out of depression is to soak up some vitamin D the natural way - through sitting in the sunshine. There is a connection between having sufficient vitamin D and having less depression. Rather than having it in a pill form soak up the natural way - the way God intended it to be. A good fifteen to twenty minutes in the sun each day should be enough to give you the vitamin D you need.

10. **Give meditation a try:** It is also worth giving meditation a try in order to learn how to relax. While learning to meditate takes time and effort, it is effort well placed as it can make your mind more peaceful and positive in its outlook. Buy a book, or DVD about meditation or join a local group so that you can practice it with other people. Mastering the technique of meditation can also aid you to bring your depression under control. If you are able to turn negative thoughts out of your mind and put it to rest then you are already half way there.

11. **Keep a journal:** If you are going through depression, it might be worth keeping a journal about your feelings, emotions and physical conditions. Your day to day observation may hold the key to how you can get out of depression. Perhaps a detailed journal can provide insight into how you can avoid a relapse.

12. **Tackle the cause:** If you think you know what is behind your depression, it can help to write down the problem, it could be financial worries, the loss of a loved one, breakdown of a relationship, end of a marriage or your spouse being sick. Once you have identified the cause think of the things you could do to tackle it. Pick the best things to do and try them out but do discuss them with your therapist, close family and friends.

13. **The power of music or sounds:** In order to relax your mind and to put yourself in a more positive state of mind it is worth giving music a try. Try keeping a CD or an i-pod full of happy, positive or upbeat music that will help you feel better. It is also worth having a CD of iPod full of relaxing sounds such as the sound of the ocean, a bubbling brook of water, birds singing in

the morning. Try something new like taking classes in Tibetean bowl sound healing.

14. **Get creative**: During times of depression in order to keep busy its worth being creative whether that means doing some embroidery, dress making, making jewellery, doing some wood work or even planting some flowers in your garden. Anything that takes your mind off your problems and gets you busy will help you pull out of depression and make you feel better.

15. **Exercise:** In addition to running try, you could join the gym, an aerobics, Pilates, yoga, dance or swimming group where you can go once or twice a week. The exercise and socialization could both help you tackle your depression.

16. **Laughter:** When you laugh the world laughs with you and when you cry you cry alone. This is another important saying to remember. You need to remind yourself to keep laughing even when you are going through the darkest of days. The ability to laugh and enjoy things is as important as the ability to go for a walk and do some exercise. So read a book of jokes, watch a funny movie, find something funny to do or find some happy funny people to hang out with.

17. **Keep hopeful:** Its important to keep reminding yourself on a daily basis that: many other people have had depression; even though right now it doesn't seem possible but you will eventually come out of it.; and, depression can sometimes be helpful – you may come out of it stronger and better able to cope. It can help you to see situations and relationships more

clearly. One of the things you can do is write down on a piece of paper that - many people have had / still have depression and I will eventually come out of it. When you feel sad or low you can look at this piece of paper and reaffirm the fact that you will come out off it.

18. **Depression can be a new beginning:** Although right now you are suffering from depression there may be a silver lining to this dark cloud. You may be able to make important decisions and changes in your life, which you have avoided in the past. It may be getting out of a bad relationship, it could be the need to change a job you are dissatisfied with or it could be about starting up a new business. But depression may give you the impetus to make these changes.

19. **Guided self-help:** There are a number ways to carry out guided self-help: self-help books using Cognitive Behavioral Therapy; self help computer programs or the Internet. You could even join an online group of people going through the same problem as yourself. So there are a number of things you can do in terms of self-help to recover from depression.

20. **Learn to love yourself:** One way to help solve your depression problem is to learn to love yourself warts and all. This also means that you learn to look after yourself and pamper yourself. Go for a spa once a month, dress well, eat well and sleep properly. More importantly it is worth instilling a sense of self-worth and self-esteem in yourself. Its only when you love yourself that others will be able to love and appreciate you. Spend a couple of minutes each day thinking about why

you deserve to be loved by yourself and others. I am certain you will find plenty of reasons why you should be loved.

8. Frequently asked questions

This chapter will deal with some of the most frequently asked questions we receive about the running therapy - plain old running or jogging actually. We hope they will be of some use for those of you who take up running and enjoy the process.

Question 1 - Should I consult a healthcare professional before running?
Answer - Yes, by all means, if you have been suffering from depression for a while now you should consult your local healthcare professional as to whether they would allow you to start running. Perhaps they feel that you need to delay running by a few weeks or they may feel that you are well up for this type of exercise and that it would benefit you.

Question 2 – Will I lose weight by running?
Answer - Yes, you can lose weight by running but its also dependent on how much you eat. Slow endurance training burns fat instead of sugars and carbohydrates and that is how you lose weight over time. But you can also gain some muscle and therefore have little to no change on the scale. However, running combined with a proper diet can help you reach a healthy weight and then maintain that weight.

Question 3 - How many miles/kilometers should I run?

Answer - This really varies with each individual while some people can run 4-5 miles a day others might only make it once around the block. It depends on your current fitness level, your physical condition, your body weight etc. The advice is to start small and build your running pace gradually. Consult a heath professional, therapist or physical trainer before starting. Start running say for about 10-15 minutes the first day and after 5 minutes of running take a minute or two of break. As you get into the flow of running then perhaps you can manage interrupted runs for longer periods of time.

Question 4 - Should I make big or little steps while running?

Answer - It's good to make short passes (high cadence). That will let your body work harder and stimulate your fat burning. As a starting point, 180 steps per minute is nice cadence. Perhaps once you start getting into the habit of running and are able to run for longer distances then you can manage longer runs and bigger steps.

Question 5 - Should I breathe through my nose or mouth?

Answer – Breathing through your mouth is the easiest and best way to start initially. If you are an experienced runner you can breathe through your nose and exhale through your mouth again.

Question 6 – Can I also additional sports besides running?

Answer – Yes you can. It is advised though to take one day off after you have walked so your muscles and tendons recover. You can take up a range of other exercises with running such as swimming, Pilates, aerobics, yoga, zumba or even dancing.

Question 7 - Can I run with my old running shoes?
Answer - When your running shoes are not older than two years and you have not run more than 2000 km with them, you can use them for training. If you do not have running shoes then it is advisable to purchase them in a store specialized in running shoes where they look very closely at the way you run and then recommend the right shoes.

Question 8 - What type of clothes should I be wearing?
Answer - you should be wearing clothes that give you room to breath in - a t-shirt that is loose, running shorts or trousers.

Question 9 - Should I be running after or before a meal?
Answer - You should always endeavor to run before a meal or at least two hours after a meal has been finished. Its better if you run on an empty stomach or run after the food has been digested. However, its is crucial to carry water with you in order to stay hydrated in order to prevent a heat stroke or heat exhaustion.

Question 10 - How many days a week should I run?
Answer - You should run as much or as little as you would like. I think initially you may just be running a couple of times a week but perhaps as you build up stamina you could run every day or 4-5 times a week.

Join our exclusive mailing list and we will send you a free eBook present.

www.TMApublishing.com

You might like:
AGING BACKWARDS Prevent Premature Aging and Look 10 Years Younger *by* Dominique Kaneza

Printed in Great Britain
by Amazon